If *da Vinci* painted a DINOSAUR

Written by **AMY NEWBOLD**
Pictures by **GREG NEWBOLD**

TILBURY HOUSE PUBLISHERS, THOMASTON, MAINE

If you drew a dinosaur,
you might start with an oval body,

then add a head and four legs.

You could draw triangles down
its back and add a spiky tail.

3.

But if Leonardo Da Vinci drew
a dinosaur, it might look like . . .

THIS!

There is more than one way to draw or paint a dinosaur.

Edgar Degas draws pastel dancers turning playful pirouettes.

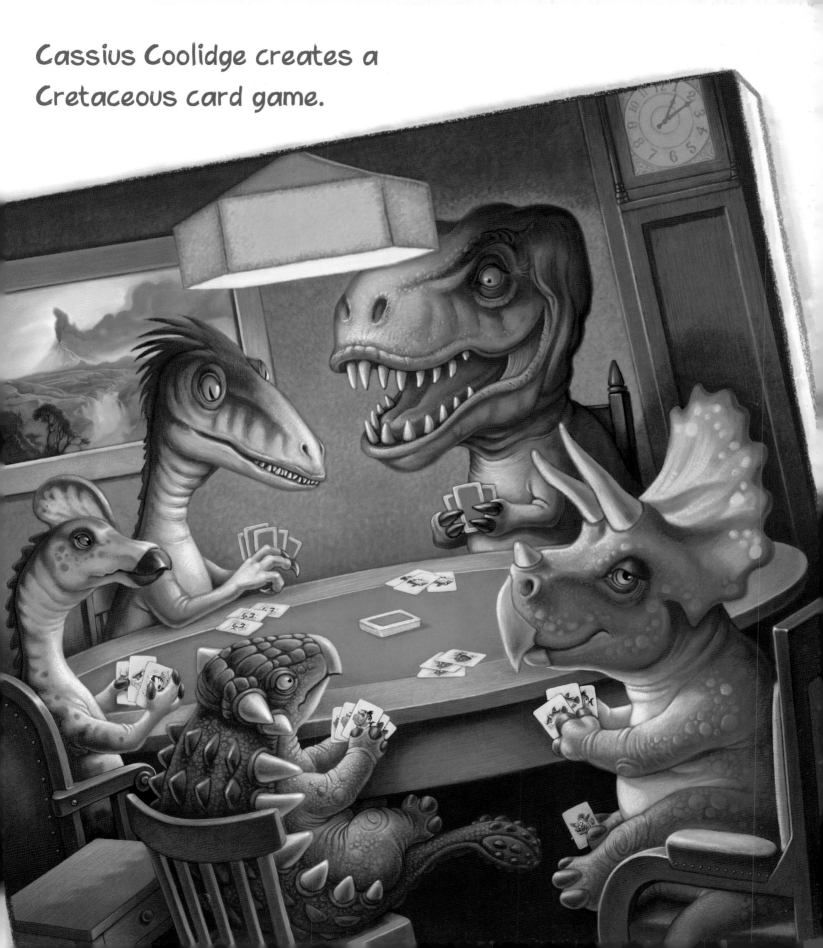

Cassius Coolidge creates a Cretaceous card game.

Do you see
dinosaurs surfing
Katsushika
Hokusai's
giant wave?

Dinosaurs stop to smell the flowers in Mary Cassatt's garden

and graze in Grandma Moses's green valley.

Parrots play peek-a-boo in Frida Kahlo's portrait.

Qi Baishi's dinosaur washes through inky bamboo.

SNIPETTY SNIP!

The paper dinosaurs
of Henri Matisse
tumble across a wall.

STOMP, STOMP, STAMP!
Three-toed tracks surround Andy Warhol's dinosaur soup.

How many dinosaurs hide in
Diego Rivera's lilies?

Franz Marc
paints a herd
of brilliant blue.

Dinosaurs leap and play in a
painting by Harrison Begay,

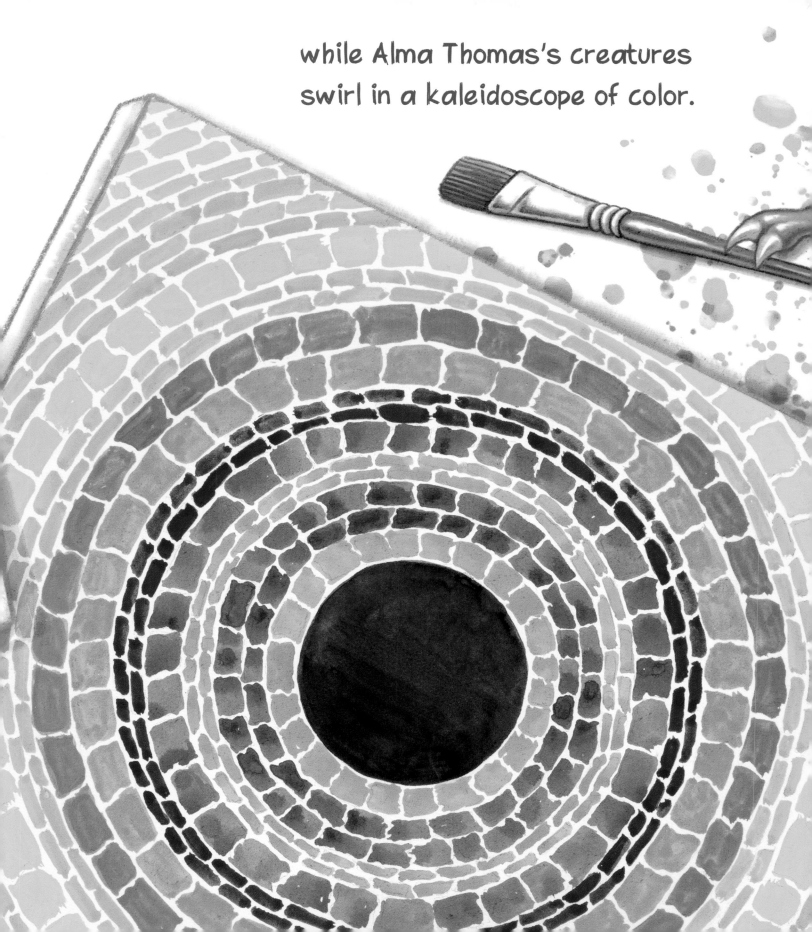

while Alma Thomas's creatures swirl in a kaleidoscope of color.

A Jurassic jazz band makes the dinosaurs of Aaron Douglas swing.

Who basks under Mark Rothko's prehistoric sun?

With triangles and squares, Loïs Mailou Jones shapes her ceratopsian mask.

Dinosaurs roam
Marguerite Zorach's
curving landscape.

BOOM! CRASH! CRUNK!

Here comes a dinosaur by Edvard Munch!

If a dinosaur sat for a portrait by
Leonardo da Vinci, it would be . . .

Copy this page and make your own.

Meet the Artists

The artists in this book came from all walks of life. Some were well-off, some were poor. Some received extensive art education, while others were self-taught. All of them persevered through great challenges to develop a strong artistic voice. Greg's paintings were inspired by each artist's unique style. When he based an illustration on a specific masterpiece, that painting is mentioned in the information below.

 **Leonardo da Vinci** (1452–1519) drew, painted, created designs for flying machines, and studied anatomy and geology. As a teenager, he was apprenticed to an art studio in Italy. He added light, shadow, and perspective in his work to create a dimension that other artists of the time were missing. His skill at drawing and painting people shows in *The Vitruvian Man* and *Mona Lisa*. Leonardo suggested that young artists "should first learn perspective, then the proportions of objects."

 Edgar Degas (1834–1917) was born in Paris, France. His mother died when he was thirteen. Edgar spent hours in the Louvre Museum, copying famous paintings. As his career progressed, he abandoned historical subjects to paint scenes from modern life, including jockeys and ballerinas. Unlike most Impressionists, with whom he exhibited, he didn't like painting in nature. Degas would draw the same subject repeatedly, working to perfect movements and gestures. He said, "Drawing is not what you see, but what you must make others see."

 Cassius Marcellus Coolidge (1844–1934) was raised on a New York farm and studied art in New York City. He was hired to paint pictures for calendars and created scenes of dogs attending baseball games and dancing to violins. His painting *A Friend in Need* shows dogs playing poker. Although his paintings garnered little critical acclaim while he was alive, they provide a humorous take on traditionally male activities.

 **Katsushika Hokusai** (1760–1849), who began drawing at age six, changed his name multiple times. In Japan, artists joined schools to study and produce their art. When Hokusai's art departed from the style of his school, he was asked to leave. This was humiliating, but it also freed his art from formal constraints and, he said, "motivated the development of my artistic style." Hokusai painted traditional Japanese figures and made a series of woodcut prints called *Thirty-Six Views of Mount Fuji*. The most famous of these prints is *The Great Wave off Kanagawa*.

 **Mary Cassatt** (1844–1926) grew up in Pennsylvania. Dissatisfied with her American art school, she convinced her parents to let her go to Paris. The École des Beaux Arts in France did not allow women students, so Mary had to find artists who would teach her. She often walked by a dealer's shop and looked at the work of Edgar Degas. "It changed my life," she said. "I saw art then as I wanted to see it." Her career was slow to develop, and she considered giving up. When Degas invited her to exhibit with the Impressionists, she embraced the style and became successful. Her art often depicts mothers and children.

Grandma Moses (1860–1961), born Anna Mary Robertson, grew up on a farm in New York, married Thomas Moses, and raised a large family. Anna made quilts and embroidered pictures. In her seventies, when arthritis made embroidery painful, she switched to painting. Her paintings are called Naïve art because she did not follow traditional rules of perspective. Nicknamed "Grandma Moses" by an art reviewer, she had a prolific career, producing nearly 1,600 paintings. Grandma Moses loved to paint scenes from her childhood farm life. She said, "Anyone that wants to paint can paint," and as if to prove it she went on painting until her death at age 101.

Frida Kahlo (1907–1954) suffered multiple fractures in an accident at age eighteen. While she recovered, her parents hung an easel above her hospital bed so that she could paint. She decided to become an artist and was encouraged by Diego Rivera, whom she later married. Frida endured many surgeries during her life. She coped with her disabilities by painting her chronic pain in self-portraits, sometimes including her parrots and monkeys. Categorized by some as a Surrealist painter, Frida said, "I really don't know if my paintings are surrealistic or not, but I do know that they are the most honest expression of myself." When she finally had a solo exhibit in her native Mexico, she was so ill her doctors told her not to attend the opening. She went anyway, in her hospital bed.

Qi Baishi (1864–1957) was from a peasant family. At age fourteen, too sickly to work on the family farm, he began teaching himself art. As he developed his skills, he found professional artists to mentor him. Qi followed Chinese painting traditions but created a unique use of bold brush strokes, bright colors, and free-flowing design. Baishi painted opera performers, family portraits, shrimp, and flowers. He liked his landscape paintings the best. He said, "The excellence of a painting lies in its being alike, yet unlike. Too much likeness flatters the vulgar taste; too much unlikeness deceives the world."

Henri Matisse (1869–1954) studied law until illness forced him to leave school. He began painting during his recovery. Rejected from art school in France, he studied at an artist's studio instead. Because he liked unnaturally bright colors, critics called him a Fauvist, or wild beast. During World War II, in Nazi-occupied France, Matisse moved repeatedly to escape the bombing. After the war he became wheelchair-bound and found painting difficult, but he did not give up. He once said, "There are flowers everywhere for those who want to see them." Matisse used paper painted by his assistants to make cutouts for large-scale scenes and murals. He continued creating art until his death in 1954.

Andy Warhol (1928–1987) was born in Pittsburgh to Slovakian immigrant parents who named him Andrew Warhola. His mother did not speak much English. When his coal miner father died, thirteen-year-old Andy worked odd jobs to help the family. A childhood disease left his skin blotchy, and kids made fun of him. Andy loved comics, magazines, and drawing. While working as a commercial artist, he changed his last name to Warhol and experimented with silk screening and mass production. A friend suggested that he paint something ordinary, so Warhol created images of thirty-two varieties of Campbell's Soup. He became a leader in Pop Art and was known for colorful screen print portraits. Warhol challenged the idea that only fine art could be in galleries and museums. He said, "An artist ought to be able to change his style without feeling bad."

Diego Rivera (1886–1957) studied art as a child in Mexico. He spent a decade in France and created many Cubist paintings. Frustrated that his art was only accessible to wealthy people, he changed his style and began painting public murals in Mexico and the United States. He painted scenes of Mexican history, everyday life, social inequality, and industrialization. He said, "An artist is above all a human being…. If the artist can't feel everything that humanity feels…, if he won't put down his magic brush and head the fight against the oppressor, then he isn't a great artist."

Franz Marc (1880–1916) experimented with art styles from a young age in Munich, Germany. He began painting realistically but later became an Abstract Expressionist. Marc thought colors were symbolic: Blue was masculine, yellow was feminine, and red was the sometimes violent physical world. As his career progressed, he painted animals, as in his work titled *The Large Blue Horses*. He said, "Art is nothing but the expression of our dream; the more we surrender to it the closer we get to the inner truth of things." When World War I began, Marc enlisted in the military and was killed in action in France at the age of thirty-six.

Aaron Douglas (1899–1979) was an African American artist and teacher who knew from his childhood in Kansas that art was his calling. Moving to New York, he became involved in the Harlem Renaissance. Layered silhouettes create depth in his flat painting style, in which the influences of Modernism, African art, and ancient Egyptian art are visible. Douglas's scenes of the African American experience focus on themes of work and struggle with larger-than-life, stylized human figures. Visual references to slavery and oppression appear with symbols of hope in his work. He wrote to poet Langston Hughes, "Let's bare our arms and plunge them deep through laughter, through pain, through sorrow, through hope, through disappointment, into the very depths of our people and drag forth material crude, rough, neglected. Then let's sing it, dance it, write it, paint it."

Harrison Begay (1914?–2012), a Navajo artist, was born in autumn, but the date was never recorded. He used November 15, 1914 as his birthdate, but some people say he was born in 1917. Life was hard on his family's Arizona sheep ranch. After his mother died, seven-year-old Harrison was sent to a boarding school. His education was interrupted by illness, changing schools, and visits home. Harrison said of his early life, "My main happiness and joy was being around the little ranch with the little lambs and little baby billy goats." After serving in the Army during World War II, Begay began painting full time. He used gouache and watercolor to create scenes from Native American life, including planting corn, weaving rugs, and performing traditional dances and ceremonies. His animal paintings, like the untitled picture of two deer running, have sensitivity and grace. Begay used a flat style of painting, keeping his figures two-dimensional with simple backgrounds.

Alma Woodsey Thomas (1891–1978) was an African American artist born in racially segregated Georgia. In 1907 her family moved to Washington, D.C. to escape the Jim Crow laws and racial tensions of the Deep South. Alma had a talent for art and became Howard University's first fine arts graduate. She taught junior high for thirty-five years before beginning her painting career in earnest at age seventy. Alma drew her Abstract Expressionist shapes in pencil before painting them in bright color patterns. She said, "The use of color in my paintings is of paramount importance to me. Through color I have sought to concentrate on beauty and happiness, rather than on man's inhumanity to man." Her Earth paintings show flowers from an aerial view, and her Space paintings, inspired by the U.S. space program, include one called *The Eclipse*. She was the first African American woman to have a solo art exhibit at the Whitney Museum of American Art in New York.

Mark Rothko (1903–1970) was born Marcus Rothkowitz in what is now Latvia. His family moved to the United States and settled in Oregon. He studied at Yale University before starting his art career. Rothko painted in a succession of art styles, including Surrealism, before finding his rhythm in large, colorful, rectangular Abstract Expressionist paintings. His paintings show feelings rather than representing a particular subject. He said, "I'm interested only in expressing basic human emotions—tragedy, ecstasy, doom, and so on—and the fact that lots of people break down and cry when confronted with my pictures shows that I communicate those basic human emotions." Rothko wanted his paintings hung low to the ground so that viewers would feel as if they were entering the painting.

Loïs Mailou Jones (1905–1998) was born in Boston, Massachusetts. She began drawing at the age of three and grew up to become an award-winning artist and successful college professor. Loïs painted everything from landscapes to portraits. She found freedom from racial prejudice when visiting France. She used her knowledge of African art in her paintings, creating beautiful abstracts. Loïs studied mask making and created costumes and textiles. Visits to Haiti inspired more color in her work. While living in Washington, D.C., Jones formed an artist group known as "Little Paris" that included fellow artist Alma Thomas. She said, "The wonderful thing about being an artist is that there's no end to creative expression. Painting is my life; my life is painting."

Marguerite Thompson Zorach (1887–1968) grew up in California and studied art in Paris, where she was influenced by the bright colors of the Fauvists and the modern shapes of the Cubists. After marrying fellow artist William Zorach, she spent most of her adult life in New York. She and William called their home the "Post-Impressionist Studio" and exhibited their work there. Together they bought a summer property in Maine, where Marguerite painted the scenery. She said about her art, "I feel complete freedom to take any liberties with form and space." Lacking uninterrupted time to paint when her children were young, she began creating textiles, batiks, and embroidery. Later, she became a leading American Modernist painter.

Edvard Munch (1863–1944) lost both his mother and his sister to illness as a boy in Norway. He studied engineering but decided to become an artist. In Paris, Munch was influenced by the post-Impressionist painters. He returned to Norway and began a series of paintings called *The Frieze of Life*, which included his famous painting *The Scream*. Munch used bright colors and strong lines to create the iconic image, making four different versions with paints and pastels. Munch's art showed the thoughts and feelings of his subjects more than their appearance. He said, "Nature is not only all that is visible to the eye ... it also includes the inner pictures of the soul." His artwork is both Symbolist and Expressionist.

Meet the Dinosaurs

The art in this book was inspired by the following dinosaurs:

Leonardo da Vinci: *Microraptor, Maiasaura*

Edgar Degas: *Ballerinasaurus imaginarius*

Cassius Coolidge (clockwise from top right): *Tyrannosaurus rex, Triceratops, Ankylosaurus, Corythosaurus, Troodon*

Katsushika Hokusai: *Plesiosaur*

Mary Cassatt: *Maiasaura*

Grandma Moses (top to bottom): *Pteranodon, Apatosaurus, Triceratops, Stegosaurus*

Frida Kahlo: *Velociraptor*

Qi Baishi: *Mei long*

Henri Matisse (clockwise from top right): *Triceratops, Stegosaurus, Allosaurus, Brontosaurus*

Andy Warhol: *theropod tracks*

Diego Rivera: *Compsognathus*

Franz Marc: *Parasaurolophus*

Harrison Begay: *Gallimimus*

Alma Thomas: *Dinosauria perspectus*

Aaron Douglas (clockwise from top right): *Brachiosaurus, Triceratops, Parasaurolophus, Plateosaurus, Stegosaurus, Apatosaurus, Torvosaurus*

Mark Rothko: *The K-T Boundary*

Loïs Mailou Jones: *Styracosaurus*

Marguerite Zorach (left to right): *Diplodocus, Triceratops, Albertosaurus, Hypsilophodon*

Edvard Munch: *Giganotosaurus*

Greg Newbold's Advice for Artists

Developing your unique artistic style and voice
takes work, so keep practicing. Here are three tips:

1. Draw.

Drawing is magic, and it's the best way to improve your art. Try to draw exactly what you see. Look for big shapes before you add details. Draw an object from different angles to develop perspective. Carry a sketchbook and draw all the time. Once you can draw realistically, you will be able to make real objects look however you want. Simplify shapes. Stylize and distort things. Merge objects for fun.

2. Explore.

Artists undertake long journeys to discover their styles. On your journey, experiment with acrylic paints, watercolors, charcoals, pastel chalks, colored pencils, or oil paints. Try surfaces like paper, canvas, cardboard, metal, or wood. Combine materials and methods to find out how they respond to each other. Maybe you will like painting on collaged magazine clippings or printed fabric. Glue objects into your art and paint around or on top of them.

3. Have Fun!

With each color or brush stroke you apply, let the picture suggest what to do next. Trust your vision. There is no right or wrong way to make art, only ways that work or don't work. If your picture doesn't turn out quite the way you wanted, figure out what worked well and use that knowledge in the future. Be inspired by other artists, but don't compare your work with theirs. They are not you!

Good luck on your artistic journey!

As a child, AMY NEWBOLD played with plastic dinosaurs in the backyard sandbox with her siblings. She learned to read at age four and has been reading and writing ever since. Amy once surprised her kids with a weekend trip out of state to visit a *Tyrannosaurus rex* named Sue. Studying so many artists for this book made her want to pick up a paintbrush. Although she once fell asleep in art history class, she has always loved art, museums, and museum gift shops. Amy enjoys road trips, hiking in the mountains near her Utah home, and really good chocolate. Her favorite dinosaur is Stegosaurus. She is the author of *If Picasso Painted a Snowman*.

One Christmas morning, GREG NEWBOLD unwrapped a box of clay and paints instead of the fancy plastic dinosaur set he had dreamed of. The box included a super-cool dinosaur book and a note from Santa saying he believed Greg would have more fun making his own creatures. Santa was right. Greg made and painted his own dinosaur set and has been drawing, painting, and making things ever since. As an award-winning illustrator, he especially enjoys making picture books with his wife, Amy, including this book and *If Picasso Painted a Snowman*.

In memory of Kevin.
—A.N.

For kids young and old who love drawing, dinosaurs,
and drawing dinosaurs. With special thanks to my
friend Yong Chen for the beautiful Chinese calligraphy.
—G.N.

Tilbury House Publishers
www.tilburyhouse.com

Text © 2018 by Amy Newbold
Illustrations © 2018 by Greg Newbold

Hardcover ISBN 978-088448-667-1
Paperback ISBN 978-0-88448-668-8

Hardcover: 15 16 17 18 19 20 XXX 10 9 8 7 6 5 4 3 2 1
Paperback: 5 4 3 2 1

Library of Congress Control Number: 2018945507

Designed by Frame25 Productions
Printed in Canada

REIMAGINED MASTERPIECES

"It took me a whole lifetime to paint like a child."
–Pablo Picasso

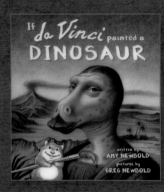

What might a snowman, dinosaur, or monster look like if it were painted by Salvador Dali or Georgia O'Keeffe or Vincent van Gogh? With Amy and Greg Newbold as guides, that simple question opens a door into the shapeshifting world of art and imagination.

"Such a treat!"
—Children's Book Council

"An inviting introduction to a range of important painters."
—School Library Journal

"Those interested in art are going to be thrilled."
—Librarian's Quest

"The big, brightly colored original illustrations range from evocative to downright authentic-looking."
—Booklist

"Art history with a little smile."
—Kirkus Reviews

"A memorable introduction to famed works of art."
—Publishers Weekly

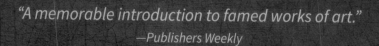

TILBURY HOUSE
PUBLISHERS

www.tilburyhouse.com

PICTURE BOOK/ART HISTORY

$9.95
ISBN 978-0-88448-668-8
50995>
9 780884 486688